Tumbling
Goalbook

© Dream Co Publishing 2023

ISBN 978-0-9951317-2-9

All rights reserved. No part of this publication may be reproduced, stored in a retrieval system, or transmitted, in any form or by any means, electronic, mechanical, photocopying, recording or otherwise, without the prior written permission of the publisher. The only exception is brief quotations for the purpose of printed reviews.

Contents:

Info	page 3
Encouraging quotes	page 4
Yearly Training Goals and outcomes	page 6
Training Goals and outcomes	page 10
Competition Goals, Scores and Acheivements	page 68
Overall scores	page 98

Tumbling Info:

Name: _____

Age: _____

Level: _____

Club: _____

Coach/es: _____

Favorite skill/s: _____

_____

Favorite apparatus/s: _____

_____

Favorite gymnast who inspires you: _____

_____

Favorite leotard: _____

_____

Inspirational words or quotes:

_____
_____
_____
_____
_____
_____
_____
_____
_____
_____
_____
_____
_____
_____
_____
_____
_____

Inspirational words or quotes:

My Yearly Training Goals:

Date: _____

_____
_____
_____
_____
_____
_____
_____
_____
_____
_____
_____
_____
_____
_____
_____

 You can do it!

My Yearly Training Outcomes:

Date: _____

_____
_____
_____
_____
_____
_____
_____
_____
_____
_____
_____
_____
_____
_____
_____

 Go for gold!

My Yearly Training Goals:

Date: _____

_____

_____

_____

_____

_____

_____

_____

_____

_____

_____

_____

_____

_____

_____

_____

  Dreams are possible

My Yearly Training Outcomes:

Date: _____

_____
_____
_____
_____
_____
_____
_____
_____
_____
_____
_____
_____
_____
_____
_____

 Flipping out is fun!

My Training Goals:

Date: _____

Apparatus: _____

_____

_____

_____

Apparatus: _____

_____

_____

_____

Apparatus: _____

_____

_____

_____

Extra comments: _____

_____

_____

 If you don't try – you won't know what you're actually capable of

My Training Outcomes:

Date: _____

Apparatus: _____

_____

_____

_____

Apparatus: _____

_____

_____

_____

Apparatus: _____

_____

_____

_____

Extra comments: _____

_____

_____

 You're a star!

My Training Goals:

Date: _____

Apparatus: _____

_____

_____

_____

Apparatus: _____

_____

_____

_____

Apparatus: _____

_____

_____

_____

Extra comments: _____

_____

_____

 Don't give up!

My Training Outcomes:

Date: _____

Apparatus: _____

_____
_____
_____

Apparatus: _____

_____
_____
_____

Apparatus: _____

_____
_____
_____

Extra comments: _____

_____
_____
_____

 Train like a champion

My Training Goals:

Date: _____

Apparatus: _____

_____

_____

_____

Apparatus: _____

_____

_____

_____

Apparatus: _____

_____

_____

_____

Extra comments: _____

_____

_____

 Aim as high as the stars!

My Training Outcomes:

Date: _____

Apparatus: _____

_____

_____

_____

Apparatus: _____

_____

_____

_____

Apparatus: _____

_____

_____

_____

Extra comments: _____

_____

_____

 You're a star!

My Training Goals:

Date: _____

Apparatus: _____

_____
_____
_____

Apparatus: _____

_____
_____
_____

Apparatus: _____

_____
_____
_____

Extra comments: _____

_____
_____

 Run towards a challenge not away from it

My Training Outcomes:

Date: _____

Apparatus: _____

_____

_____

_____

Apparatus: _____

_____

_____

_____

Apparatus: _____

_____

_____

_____

Extra comments: _____

_____

_____

 You got this!

My Training Goals:

Date: _____

Apparatus: _____

_____

_____

_____

Apparatus: _____

_____

_____

_____

Apparatus: _____

_____

_____

_____

Extra comments: _____

_____

_____

 You're amazing

My Training Outcomes:

Date: _____

Apparatus: _____

_____

_____

_____

Apparatus: _____

_____

_____

_____

Apparatus: _____

_____

_____

_____

Extra comments: _____

_____

_____

 Believe – achieve

My Training Goals:

Date: _____

Apparatus: _____

_____

_____

_____

Apparatus: _____

_____

_____

_____

Apparatus: _____

_____

_____

_____

Extra comments: _____

_____

_____

My Training Outcomes:

Date: _____

Apparatus: _____

_____

_____

_____

Apparatus: _____

_____

_____

_____

Apparatus: _____

_____

_____

_____

Extra comments: _____

_____

_____

 Be strong. And smile!

My Training Goals:

Date: _____

Apparatus: _____

_____

_____

_____

Apparatus: _____

_____

_____

_____

Apparatus: _____

_____

_____

_____

Extra comments: _____

_____

_____

 You can do it!

My Training Outcomes:

Date: _____

Apparatus: _____

_____

_____

_____

Apparatus: _____

_____

_____

_____

Apparatus: _____

_____

_____

_____

Extra comments: _____

_____

_____

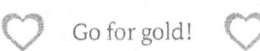

My Training Goals:

Date: _____

Apparatus: _____

_____

_____

_____

Apparatus: _____

_____

_____

_____

Apparatus: _____

_____

_____

_____

Extra comments: _____

_____

_____

 Dreams are possible!

My Training Outcomes:

Date: _____

Apparatus: _____

_____

_____

_____

Apparatus: _____

_____

_____

_____

Apparatus: _____

_____

_____

_____

Extra comments: _____

_____

_____

 Flipping out is fun!

My Training Goals:

Date: _____

Apparatus: _____

_____
_____
_____

Apparatus: _____

_____
_____
_____

Apparatus: _____

_____
_____
_____

Extra comments: _____
_____
_____

 Don't give up!

My Training Outcomes:

Date: _____

Apparatus: _____

_____

_____

_____

Apparatus: _____

_____

_____

_____

Apparatus: _____

_____

_____

_____

Extra comments: _____

_____

_____

 Train like a champion

My Training Goals:

Date: _____

Apparatus: _____

_____

_____

_____

Apparatus: _____

_____

_____

_____

Apparatus: _____

_____

_____

_____

Extra comments: _____

_____

_____

 Tumble tumble tumble!

My Training Outcomes:

Date: _____

Apparatus: _____

_____

_____

_____

Apparatus: _____

_____

_____

_____

Apparatus: _____

_____

_____

_____

Extra comments: _____

_____

_____

You're a star!

My Training Goals:

Date: _____

Apparatus: _____

_____
_____
_____

Apparatus: _____

_____
_____
_____

Apparatus: _____

_____
_____
_____

Extra comments: _____

_____
_____

 Tumbling counts as flying!

My Training Outcomes:

Date: _____

Apparatus: _____

_____
_____
_____

Apparatus: _____

_____
_____
_____

Apparatus: _____

_____
_____
_____

Extra comments: _____

_____
_____

 I love tumbling!

My Training Goals:

Date: _____

Apparatus: _____

_____
_____
_____

Apparatus: _____

_____
_____
_____

Apparatus: _____

_____
_____
_____

Extra comments: _____

_____
_____

 If you don't try – you won't know
what you're actually capable of

My Training Outcomes:

Date: _____

Apparatus: _____

_____
_____
_____

Apparatus: _____

_____
_____
_____

Apparatus: _____

_____
_____
_____

Extra comments: _____

_____
_____

 You got this!

My Training Goals:

Date: _____

Apparatus: _____

_____

_____

_____

Apparatus: _____

_____

_____

_____

Apparatus: _____

_____

_____

_____

Extra comments: _____

_____

_____

♡ Tumble tracks are the best!

My Training Outcomes:

Date: _____

Apparatus: _____

_____

_____

_____

Apparatus: _____

_____

_____

_____

Apparatus: _____

_____

_____

_____

Extra comments: _____

_____

_____

♡ Don't forget to have fun ♡

My Training Goals:

Date: _____

Apparatus: _____

_____
_____
_____

Apparatus: _____

_____
_____
_____

Apparatus: _____

_____
_____
_____

Extra comments: _____
_____
_____

 Run towards a challenge, not away from it!

My Training Outcomes:

Date: _____

Apparatus: _____

_____

_____

_____

Apparatus: _____

_____

_____

_____

Apparatus: _____

_____

_____

_____

Extra comments: _____

_____

_____

 Today is your day!

My Training Goals:

Date: _____

Apparatus: _____

_____
_____
_____

Apparatus: _____

_____
_____
_____

Apparatus: _____

_____
_____
_____

Extra comments: _____

_____
_____

 You're amazing

My Training Outcomes:

Date: _____

Apparatus: _____

_____

_____

_____

Apparatus: _____

_____

_____

_____

Apparatus: _____

_____

_____

_____

Extra comments: _____

_____

_____

 Believe – achieve

My Training Goals:

Date: _____

Apparatus: _____

_____

_____

_____

Apparatus: _____

_____

_____

_____

Apparatus: _____

_____

_____

_____

Extra comments: _____

_____

_____

♡ ...it's a gymnast thing ♡

My Training Outcomes:

Date: _____

Apparatus: _____

_____

_____

_____

Apparatus: _____

_____

_____

_____

Apparatus: _____

_____

_____

_____

Extra comments: _____

_____

_____

 Be strong. And smile!

My Training Goals:

Date: _____

Apparatus: _____

_____

_____

_____

Apparatus: _____

_____

_____

_____

Apparatus: _____

_____

_____

_____

Extra comments: _____

_____

_____

 You can do it!

My Training Outcomes:

Date: _____

Apparatus: _____

_____
_____
_____

Apparatus: _____

_____
_____
_____

Apparatus: _____

_____
_____
_____

Extra comments: _____

_____
_____
_____

 Go for gold!

My Training Goals:

Date: _____

Apparatus: _____

_____
_____
_____

Apparatus: _____

_____
_____
_____

Apparatus: _____

_____
_____
_____

Extra comments: _____
_____
_____

 Dreams are possible

My Training Outcomes:

Date: _____

Apparatus: _____

_____
_____
_____

Apparatus: _____

_____
_____
_____

Apparatus: _____

_____
_____
_____

Extra comments: _____

_____
_____

 Flipping out is fun!

My Training Goals:

Date: _____

Apparatus: _____

_____
_____
_____

Apparatus: _____

_____
_____
_____

Apparatus: _____

_____
_____
_____

Extra comments: _____

_____
_____

 Don't give up!

My Training Outcomes:

Date: _____

Apparatus: _____

_____

_____

_____

Apparatus: _____

_____

_____

_____

Apparatus: _____

_____

_____

_____

Extra comments: _____

_____

_____

 Train like a champion

My Training Goals:

Date: _____

Apparatus: _____

_____

_____

_____

Apparatus: _____

_____

_____

_____

Apparatus: _____

_____

_____

_____

Extra comments: _____

_____

_____

 Aim as high as the stars!

My Training Outcomes:

Date: _____

Apparatus: _____

_____
_____
_____

Apparatus: _____

_____
_____
_____

Apparatus: _____

_____
_____
_____

Extra comments: _____

_____
_____
_____

 You're a star!

My Training Goals:

Date: _____

Apparatus: _____

_____

_____

_____

Apparatus: _____

_____

_____

_____

Apparatus: _____

_____

_____

_____

Extra comments: _____

_____

_____

♡ Tumbling upside down is fun! ♡

My Training Outcomes:

Date: _____

Apparatus: _____

_____
_____
_____

Apparatus: _____

_____
_____
_____

Apparatus: _____

_____
_____
_____

Extra comments: _____

_____
_____

 I love tumbling!

My Training Goals:

Date: _____

Apparatus: _____

_____

_____

_____

Apparatus: _____

_____

_____

_____

Apparatus: _____

_____

_____

_____

Extra comments: _____

_____

_____

 If you don't try – you won't know
what you're actually capable of

My Training Outcomes:

Date: _____

Apparatus: _____

_____

_____

_____

Apparatus: _____

_____

_____

_____

Apparatus: _____

_____

_____

_____

Extra comments: _____

_____

_____

You got this!

My Training Goals:

Date: _____

Apparatus: _____

_____

_____

_____

Apparatus: _____

_____

_____

_____

Apparatus: _____

_____

_____

_____

Extra comments: _____

_____

_____

 Power tumbling is awesome!

My Training Outcomes:

Date: _____

Apparatus: _____

_____

_____

_____

Apparatus: _____

_____

_____

_____

Apparatus: _____

_____

_____

_____

Extra comments: _____

_____

_____

 Don't forget to have fun

My Training Goals:

Date: _____

Apparatus: _____

_____

_____

_____

Apparatus: _____

_____

_____

_____

Apparatus: _____

_____

_____

_____

Extra comments: _____

_____

_____

♡ Run towards a challenge, not away from it ♡

My Training Outcomes:

Date: _____

Apparatus: _____

_____
_____
_____

Apparatus: _____

_____
_____
_____

Apparatus: _____

_____
_____
_____

Extra comments: _____

_____
_____
_____

♡ Fly like an eagle ♡

My Training Goals:

Date: _____

Apparatus: _____

_____

_____

_____

Apparatus: _____

_____

_____

_____

Apparatus: _____

_____

_____

_____

Extra comments: _____

_____

_____

 You're amazing

My Training Outcomes:

Date: _____

Apparatus: _____

_____

_____

_____

Apparatus: _____

_____

_____

_____

Apparatus: _____

_____

_____

_____

Extra comments: _____

_____

_____

 Believe – achieve

My Training Goals:

Date: _____

Apparatus: _____

_____

_____

_____

Apparatus: _____

_____

_____

_____

Apparatus: _____

_____

_____

_____

Extra comments: _____

_____

_____

 ...it's a gymnast thing

My Training Outcomes:

Date: _____

Apparatus: _____

_____
_____
_____

Apparatus: _____

_____
_____
_____

Apparatus: _____

_____
_____
_____

Extra comments: _____

_____
_____

 Be strong. And smile!

My Training Goals:

Date: _____

Apparatus: _____

_____

_____

_____

Apparatus: _____

_____

_____

_____

Apparatus: _____

_____

_____

_____

Extra comments: _____

_____

_____

♡ You can do it! ♡

My Training Outcomes:

Date: _____

Apparatus: _____

_____

_____

_____

Apparatus: _____

_____

_____

_____

Apparatus: _____

_____

_____

_____

Extra comments: _____

_____

_____

 Go for gold!

My Training Goals:

Date: _____

Apparatus: _____

_____

_____

_____

Apparatus: _____

_____

_____

_____

Apparatus: _____

_____

_____

_____

Extra comments: _____

_____

_____

♡ Dreams are possible ♡

My Training Outcomes:

Date: _____

Apparatus: _____

_____

_____

_____

Apparatus: _____

_____

_____

_____

Apparatus: _____

_____

_____

_____

Extra comments: _____

_____

_____

 Flipping out is fun!

My Training Goals:

Date: _____

Apparatus: _____

_____
_____
_____

Apparatus: _____

_____
_____
_____

Apparatus: _____

_____
_____
_____

Extra comments: _____

_____
_____

♡ Don't give up! ♡

My Training Outcomes:

Date: _____

Apparatus: _____

_____

_____

_____

Apparatus: _____

_____

_____

_____

Apparatus: _____

_____

_____

_____

Extra comments: _____

_____

_____

 Train like a champion

My Competition Goals:

Date: _____

Competition name: _____

Apparatus: _____

_____

_____

_____

Apparatus: _____

_____

_____

_____

Apparatus: _____

_____

_____

_____

Extra comments: _____

_____

Tumbling counts as flying!

My Competition Achievements:

Apparatus: _____

Score: _____

_____

_____

Apparatus: _____

Score: _____

_____

_____

Apparatus: _____

Score: _____

_____

_____

Overall score: _____

Overall outcomes: _____

_____

_____

♡ I love tumbling! ♡

My Competition Goals:

Date: _____

Competition name: _____

Apparatus: _____

_____
_____
_____

Apparatus: _____

_____
_____
_____

Apparatus: _____

_____
_____
_____

Extra comments: _____
_____

 If you don't try – you won't know what you're actually capable of

My Competition Achievements:

Apparatus: _____

Score: _____

_____

_____

Apparatus: _____

Score: _____

_____

_____

Apparatus: _____

Score: _____

_____

_____

Overall score: _____

Overall outcomes: _____

_____

_____

 You got this!

My Competition Goals:

Date: _____

Competition name: _____

Apparatus: _____

_____
_____
_____

Apparatus: _____

_____
_____
_____

Apparatus: _____

_____
_____
_____

Extra comments: _____
_____

 Tumble track tumbling is fun!

My Competition Achievements:

Apparatus: _____

Score: _____

_____

_____

Apparatus: _____

Score: _____

_____

_____

Apparatus: _____

Score: _____

_____

_____

Overall score: _____

Overall outcomes: _____

_____

_____

 Don't forget to have fun!

My Competition Goals:

Date: _____

Competition name: _____

Apparatus: _____

_____
_____
_____

Apparatus: _____

_____
_____
_____

Apparatus: _____

_____
_____
_____

Extra comments: _____

_____

 Run towards a **challenge**, not away from it

My Competition Achievements:

Apparatus: _____

Score: _____

_____

_____

Apparatus: _____

Score: _____

_____

_____

Apparatus: _____

Score: _____

_____

_____

Overall score: _____

Overall outcomes: _____

_____

_____

 Fly like an eagle!

My Competition Goals:

Date: _____

Competition name: _____

Apparatus: _____

_____
_____
_____

Apparatus: _____

_____
_____
_____

Apparatus: _____

_____
_____
_____

Extra comments: _____
_____

♡ You're amazing ♡

My Competition Achievements:

Apparatus: _____

Score: _____

_____

_____

Apparatus: _____

Score: _____

_____

_____

Apparatus: _____

Score: _____

_____

_____

Overall score: _____

Overall outcomes: _____

_____

_____

 Believe – achieve

My Competition Goals:

Date: _____

Competition name: _____

Apparatus: _____

_____

_____

_____

Apparatus: _____

_____

_____

_____

Apparatus: _____

_____

_____

_____

Extra comments: _____

_____

 ...it's a gymnast thing

My Competition Achievements:

Apparatus: _____

Score: _____

_____

_____

Apparatus: _____

Score: _____

_____

_____

Apparatus: _____

Score: _____

_____

_____

Overall score: _____

Overall outcomes: _____

_____

_____

 Be strong. And smile! ♡

My Competition Goals:

Date: _____

Competition name: _____

Apparatus: _____

_____

_____

_____

Apparatus: _____

_____

_____

_____

Apparatus: _____

_____

_____

_____

Extra comments: _____

_____

 You can do it!

My Competition Achievements:

Apparatus: _____

Score: _____

_____

_____

Apparatus: _____

Score: _____

_____

_____

Apparatus: _____

Score: _____

_____

_____

Overall score: _____

Overall outcomes: _____

_____

_____

 Go for gold!

My Competition Goals:

Date: _____

Competition name: _____

Apparatus: _____

_____
_____
_____

Apparatus: _____

_____
_____
_____

Apparatus: _____

_____
_____
_____

Extra comments: _____

_____

 Dreams are possible

My Competition Achievements:

Apparatus: _____

Score: _____

_____

_____

Apparatus: _____

Score: _____

_____

_____

Apparatus: _____

Score: _____

_____

_____

Overall score: _____

Overall outcomes: _____

_____

_____

 Flipping out is fun!

My Competition Goals:

Date: _____

Competition name: _____

Apparatus: _____

_____
_____
_____

Apparatus: _____

_____
_____
_____

Apparatus: _____

_____
_____
_____

Extra comments: _____
_____

 Don't give up!

My Competition Achievements:

Apparatus: _____

Score: _____

_____

_____

Apparatus: _____

Score: _____

_____

_____

Apparatus: _____

Score: _____

_____

_____

Overall score: _____

Overall outcomes: _____

_____

_____

 Train like a champion

My Competition Goals:

Date: _____

Competition name: _____

Apparatus: _____

_____

_____

_____

Apparatus: _____

_____

_____

_____

Apparatus: _____

_____

_____

_____

Extra comments: _____

_____

 Aim as high as the stars!

My Competition Achievements:

Apparatus: _____

Score: _____

_____

_____

Apparatus: _____

Score: _____

_____

_____

Apparatus: _____

Score: _____

_____

_____

Overall score: _____

Overall outcomes: _____

_____

_____

 You're a star!

My Competition Goals:

Date: _____

Competition name: _____

Apparatus: _____

_____
_____
_____

Apparatus: _____

_____
_____
_____

Apparatus: _____

_____
_____
_____

Extra comments: _____
_____

 Tumbling counts as flying

My Competition Achievements:

Apparatus: _____

Score: _____

_____

_____

Apparatus: _____

Score: _____

_____

_____

Apparatus: _____

Score: _____

_____

_____

Overall score: _____

Overall outcomes: _____

_____

_____

 I love tumbling!

My Competition Goals:

Date: _____

Competition name: _____

Apparatus: _____

_____

_____

_____

Apparatus: _____

_____

_____

_____

Apparatus: _____

_____

_____

_____

Extra comments: _____

_____

 If you don't try – you won't know
what you're actually capable of!

My Competition Achievements:

Apparatus: _____

Score: _____

_____

_____

Apparatus: _____

Score: _____

_____

_____

Apparatus: _____

Score: _____

_____

_____

Overall score: _____

Overall outcomes: _____

_____

_____

 You got this!

My Competition Goals:

Date: _____

Competition name: _____

Apparatus: _____

_____
_____
_____

Apparatus: _____

_____
_____
_____

Apparatus: _____

_____
_____
_____

Extra comments: _____
_____

 Tumbling is fun!

My Competition Achievements:

Apparatus: _____

Score: _____

_____

_____

Apparatus: _____

Score: _____

_____

_____

Apparatus: _____

Score: _____

_____

_____

Overall score: _____

Overall outcomes: _____

_____

_____

 You're a star!

My Competition Goals:

Date: _____

Competition name: _____

Apparatus: _____

_____

_____

_____

Apparatus: _____

_____

_____

_____

Apparatus: _____

_____

_____

_____

Extra comments: _____

_____

Aim as high as the stars!

My Competition Achievements:

Apparatus: _____

Score: _____

_____

_____

Apparatus: _____

Score: _____

_____

_____

Apparatus: _____

Score: _____

_____

_____

Overall score: _____

Overall outcomes: _____

_____

_____

 Don't forget to have fun! ♡

My Competition Goals:

Date: _____

Competition name: _____

Apparatus: _____

_____
_____
_____

Apparatus: _____

_____
_____
_____

Apparatus: _____

_____
_____
_____

Extra comments: _____
_____

 Go for it!

My Competition Achievements:

Apparatus: _____

Score: _____

_____

_____

Apparatus: _____

Score: _____

_____

_____

Apparatus: _____

Score: _____

_____

_____

Overall score: _____

Overall outcomes: _____

_____

_____

 I love tumbling!

Overall score sheet

Competition: _____

Score: _____

Competition: _____

Score: _____

Competition: _____

Score: _____

Competition: _____

Score: _____

Competition: _____

Score: _____

Competition: _____

Score: _____

Competition: _____

Score: _____

Competition: _____

Score: _____

♡ Overall score sheet ♡

Competition: _____

Score: _____

Competition: _____

Score: _____

Competition: _____

Score: _____

Competition: _____

Score: _____

Competition: _____

Score: _____

Competition: _____

Score: _____

Competition: _____

Score: _____

Competition: _____

Score: _____

www.ingramcontent.com/pod-product-compliance
Lightning Source LLC
Chambersburg PA
CBHW070436010526
44118CB00014B/2071